This book is dedicated to you.

Friend in My Head

How To Set Your Goals For Success In Life

By BIRDIE CHESSON

ISBN:
978-1-732-166226
Copyright 2019 by Birdie Chesson

FOREWARD

"She's my *Friend in my Head...*"
It's an expression that was originally coined as an emotional and mental term for a sisterhood that is based on finding common ground with a complete stranger. So you may not know me personally, but I am that friend.

I want people to be able to pursue what they really want in life and I made this book so that I can help you reach those goals. Now I can cheer you on from the sidelines.
I need encouragement too. You out there using this book helps me know that I am not alone in pursuing what I really want in my own life.

So what do *you* really want to do? How will you do it? It's *all* possible. Sometimes, all you need to do is sort it out and do it, one day at a time.
We can do it together, as friends in each others' heads.
This book is portioned like a 2-year scheduler so that you can set your goals daily, weekly, monthly and yearly here. There are encouraging words with accountability tools that can help keep you on track. The dates are blank so that you can start this book at ANY TIME of the year, as soon as TODAY. Or tomorrow.

In the back, there's a tool on how to schedule your time in general, one day at a time and a place to write any notes or revelations about yourself and your journey. We are a sisterhood.

Let's set goals together. Then set more goals and crush those too!
We've got this!
Love, Birdie. *Your friend in your Head.*

Goals

What do you really want?
Why do you want it?

Dreams and wishes become goals when written down. Plan to succeed, put it into action and it WILL become a reality.

It takes 21 days of committing to a goal to make it a habit,
After 60 days, it becomes automatic.
After 90 days, it's a real lifestyle change.
Consistency is what determines your success in whatever you want.

Go to the gym, start that business, set a sales goal and/or write that book you've always wanted to write.
YOU GOT THIS!

Don't rush and don't put too much pressure on yourself. Have fun on this journey.
Set your goals and work at it at a pace you're comfortable with...

One day at a time.

What do want to happen this year?
What will you start doing this month?

January

February

March

April

May

June

Where do you think that you will be in 6 months?

July

August

September

October

November

December

One day at a time...

Do you have your vision of what you
want yet?
Why do you want it?
What will we have to do tomorrow to
move towards what we want?

If you're not sure of what to do yet, just
start by writing about your day, like a
diary. Just write what you did that day to
see how you spend your days.

This may help you realize that either
you're living the way you want to live,
but it also may help you figure out what
you actually want to do.

Start.
Build the momentum and stay consistent.

(Don't beat yourself up if you start
the day after tomorrow)

Just start.

 Monday

 Tuesday

 Wednesday

 Thursday

 Friday

 Saturday

 Sunday

 Monday

 Tuesday

 Wednesday

 Thursday

 Friday

 Saturday

 Sunday

Monday

Tuesday

Wednesday

 Thursday

 Friday

 Saturday

 Sunday

Monday

Tuesday

Wednesday

 Thursday

 Friday

 Saturday

 Sunday

It has been about a month now, how are you doing?
If you like it, KEEP UP THE GOOD WORK!

Monday

Tuesday

Wednesday

Week Five

 Thursday

 Friday

 Saturday

 Sunday

 Monday

 Tuesday

 Wednesday

Thursday

Friday

Saturday

Sunday

 ## Monday

 ## Tuesday

 ## Wednesday

Thursday

Friday

Saturday

Sunday

Monday

Tuesday

Wednesday

 Thursday

 Friday

 Saturday

 Sunday

 Monday

 Tuesday

 Wednesday

Week Nine

Thursday

Friday

Saturday

Sunday

 Monday

 Tuesday

 Wednesday

Week Ten

 Thursday

 Friday

 Saturday

 Sunday

 Monday

 Tuesday

 Wednesday

Week Eleven

 Thursday

 Friday

 Saturday

 Sunday

 Monday

 Tuesday

 Wednesday

Week Twelve

 Thursday

 Friday

 Saturday

 Sunday

It has been about 3 months. Are you seeing results?
If not, let's look at what changes you can make NOW.

Monday

Tuesday

Wednesday

Week Thirteen

Thursday

Friday

Saturday

Sunday

Monday

Tuesday

Wednesday

Week Fourteen

 Thursday

 Friday

 Saturday

 Sunday

 Monday

 Tuesday

 Wednesday

 Thursday

 Friday

 Saturday

 Sunday

Monday

Tuesday

Wednesday

 Thursday

 Friday

 Saturday

 Sunday

 Monday

 Tuesday

 Wednesday

Thursday

Friday

Saturday

Sunday

 Monday

 Tuesday

 Wednesday

Week Eighteen

Thursday

Friday

Saturday

Sunday

 Monday

 Tuesday

 Wednesday

 Thursday

 Friday

 Saturday

 Sunday

 Monday

 Tuesday

 Wednesday

Thursday

Friday

Saturday

Sunday

Monday

Tuesday

Wednesday

 Thursday

 Friday

 Saturday

 Sunday

 Monday

 Tuesday

 Wednesday

 Thursday

 Friday

 Saturday

 Sunday

Monday

Tuesday

Wednesday

Thursday

Friday

Saturday

Sunday

 Monday

 Tuesday

 Wednesday

 Thursday

 Friday

 Saturday

 Sunday

 Monday

 Tuesday

 Wednesday

 Thursday

 Friday

 Saturday

 Sunday

 Monday

 Tuesday

 Wednesday

Thursday

Friday

Saturday

Sunday

Accountability Notes:

26 weeks have gone by.
That means, it has been half a year already!

Where are you with your goals?
Did you start towards your healthier lifestyle
yet?
Are you keeping up with your fitness goal?
Did you start that business?
Did you finish that chapter of your book?

Let's reassess. You can look at your original
planning page from the beginning of the year
to see how far you've come.

If you've let time go by, don't beat yourself up,
NOW'S the time to get back into it!

If you've continued thus far, keep up the great
work! If you've met your goal, set another one!

Everyday is an opportunity to start fresh to be,
do and have whatever you want in this life.

Let's see what we can do for the rest of the
year!

It's the middle of the year. How are you doing with your goals? Let's set our goals for the rest of the year!

July

August

September

October

November

December

 Monday

 Tuesday

 Wednesday

 Thursday

 Friday

 Saturday

 Sunday

 Monday

 Tuesday

 Wednesday

 Thursday

 Friday

 Saturday

 Sunday

 Monday

 Tuesday

 Wednesday

Week Twenty-Nine

 Thursday

 Friday

 Saturday

 Sunday

Monday

Tuesday

Wednesday

 Thursday

 Friday

 Saturday

 Sunday

 Monday

 Tuesday

 Wednesday

Thursday

Friday

Saturday

Sunday

 Monday

 Tuesday

 Wednesday

 Thursday

 Friday

 Saturday

 Sunday

 Monday

 Tuesday

 Wednesday

 Thursday

 Friday

 Saturday

 Sunday

 Monday

 Tuesday

 Wednesday

 Thursday

 Friday

 Saturday

 Sunday

 Monday

 Tuesday

 Wednesday

Thursday

Friday

Saturday

Sunday

 Monday

 Tuesday

 Wednesday

 Thursday

 Friday

 Saturday

 Sunday

Monday

Tuesday

Wednesday

 Thursday

 Friday

 Saturday

 Sunday

 Monday

 Tuesday

 Wednesday

 Thursday

 Friday

 Saturday

 Sunday

 Monday

 Tuesday

 Wednesday

 Thursday

 Friday

 Saturday

 Sunday

Monday

Tuesday

Wednesday

Thursday

Friday

Saturday

Sunday

Monday

Tuesday

Wednesday

 Thursday

 Friday

 Saturday

 Sunday

 Monday

 Tuesday

 Wednesday

 Thursday

 Friday

 Saturday

 Sunday

 Monday

 Tuesday

 Wednesday

Week Forty-Three

 Thursday

 Friday

 Saturday

 Sunday

Monday

Tuesday

Wednesday

Thursday

Friday

Saturday

Sunday

 Monday

 Tuesday

 Wednesday

 Thursday

 Friday

 Saturday

 Sunday

 Monday

 Tuesday

 Wednesday

Thursday

Friday

Saturday

Sunday

 Monday

 Tuesday

 Wednesday

 Thursday

 Friday

 Saturday

 Sunday

 Monday

 Tuesday

 Wednesday

 Thursday

 Friday

 Saturday

 Sunday

 Monday

 Tuesday

 Wednesday

 Thursday

 Friday

 Saturday

 Sunday

 Monday

 Tuesday

 Wednesday

 Thursday

 Friday

 Saturday

 Sunday

 Monday

 Tuesday

 Wednesday

Thursday

Friday

Saturday

Sunday

 Monday

 Tuesday

 Wednesday

Week Fifty-Two

 Thursday

 Friday

Saturday

 Sunday

HAPPY NEW YEAR!

You either did what you wanted for yourself last year
or you didn't.

If you did accomplish your goals,
I am so happy for you!
Now let's plan for something else you want!

If you didn't accomplish your goals,
don't be too hard on yourself.
It can be **clean slate time**! Every day is a chance to
make a better week, month and eventually your year!

Give yourself a chance to succeed.
Give yourself permission to have the life
that you deserve.
Now, what do you want to do towards that life?

We can start a new goal or keep steady
on the course from last year, consistently.

It's up to you.
Either way, we still got this!

Now that we have our goals,
Let's start this year off right!
Without too much pressure, remember that you can
do all that you've ever wanted to do.

If the goal feels too big, remember that you can
always pace yourself, focus one day at a time.

What do you want to accomplish this year?
Don't put too much pressure on yourself.
Remember, take it ONE DAY AT A TIME!

January

_____

_____

_____

February

_____

_____

_____

March

_____

_____

_____

April

_____

_____

_____

May

_____

_____

_____

June

_____

_____

_____

Let's set Goals for the rest of the year!

July

August

September

October

November

December

Monday

Tuesday

Wednesday

 Thursday

 Friday

 Saturday

 Sunday

 Monday

 Tuesday

 Wednesday

 ## Thursday

 ## Friday

 ## Saturday

 ## Sunday

Monday

Tuesday

Wednesday

 Thursday

 Friday

 Saturday

 Sunday

 Monday

 Tuesday

 Wednesday

 Thursday

 Friday

 Saturday

 Sunday

 Monday

 Tuesday

 Wednesday

 Thursday

 Friday

 Saturday

 Sunday

Monday

Tuesday

Wednesday

 Thursday

 Friday

 Saturday

 Sunday

 Monday

 Tuesday

 Wednesday

Thursday

Friday

Saturday

Sunday

 Monday

 Tuesday

 Wednesday

 Thursday

 Friday

 Saturday

 Sunday

 Monday

 Tuesday

 Wednesday

Thursday

Friday

Saturday

Sunday

 Monday

 Tuesday

 Wednesday

 Thursday

 Friday

 Saturday

 Sunday

 Monday

 Tuesday

 Wednesday

 Thursday

 Friday

 Saturday

 Sunday

Monday

Tuesday

Wednesday

 Thursday

 Friday

 Saturday

 Sunday

Monday

Tuesday

Wednesday

 Thursday

 Friday

 Saturday

 Sunday

 Monday

 Tuesday

 Wednesday

 Thursday

 Friday

 Saturday

 Sunday

 Monday

 Tuesday

 Wednesday

Thursday

Friday

Saturday

Sunday

 Monday

 Tuesday

 Wednesday

Week Sixteen

 Thursday

 Friday

 Saturday

 Sunday

 Monday

 Tuesday

 Wednesday

 Thursday

 Friday

 Saturday

 Sunday

 Monday

 Tuesday

 Wednesday

Thursday

Friday

Saturday

Sunday

Monday

Tuesday

Wednesday

Week Nineteen

 Thursday

 Friday

 Saturday

 Sunday

 Monday

 Tuesday

 Wednesday

 Thursday

 Friday

 Saturday

 Sunday

 Monday

 Tuesday

 Wednesday

 Thursday

 Friday

 Saturday

 Sunday

 Monday

 Tuesday

 Wednesday

 Thursday

 Friday

 Saturday

 Sunday

 Monday

 Tuesday

 Wednesday

 Thursday

 Friday

 Saturday

 Sunday

 Monday

 Tuesday

 Wednesday

 Thursday

 Friday

 Saturday

 Sunday

 Monday

 Tuesday

 Wednesday

 Thursday

 Friday

 Saturday

 Sunday

Monday

Tuesday

Wednesday

 Thursday

 Friday

 Saturday

 Sunday

Time for Accountability:

Another 26 weeks have gone by.
That means, it has been a year and
a half in our plans together!

Where are you with your goals?
Have you changed your lifestyle?
Are you going to the gym regularly?
Did you start your business?
Did you finish your book?

Now's the time to stay on track!

One day at a time.
Then one week strong, then a month.

Let's finish these 2 years strong!

Let's set our goals for the rest of the year!

July

August

September

October

November

December

Monday

Tuesday

Wednesday

 Thursday

 Friday

 Saturday

 Sunday

 Monday

 Tuesday

 Wednesday

 Thursday

 Friday

 Saturday

 Sunday

Monday

Tuesday

Wednesday

 Thursday

 Friday

 Saturday

 Sunday

Monday

Tuesday

Wednesday

 Thursday

 Friday

 Saturday

 Sunday

 Monday

 Tuesday

 Wednesday

 Thursday

 Friday

 Saturday

 Sunday

 Monday

 Tuesday

 Wednesday

 Thursday

 Friday

 Saturday

 Sunday

Monday

Tuesday

Wednesday

 Thursday

 Friday

 Saturday

 Sunday

Monday

Tuesday

Wednesday

 Thursday

 Friday

 Saturday

 Sunday

Monday

Tuesday

Wednesday

 Thursday

 Friday

 Saturday

 Sunday

 Monday

 Tuesday

 Wednesday

 Thursday

 Friday

 Saturday

 Sunday

Monday

Tuesday

Wednesday

 Thursday

 Friday

 Saturday

 Sunday

Monday

Tuesday

Wednesday

Thursday

Friday

Saturday

Sunday

 Monday

 Tuesday

 Wednesday

 Thursday

 Friday

 Saturday

 Sunday

Monday

Tuesday

Wednesday

 Thursday

 Friday

 Saturday

 Sunday

Monday

Tuesday

Wednesday

 Thursday

 Friday

 Saturday

 Sunday

Monday

Tuesday

Wednesday

 Thursday

 Friday

 Saturday

 Sunday

 Monday

 Tuesday

 Wednesday

 Thursday

 Friday

 Saturday

 Sunday

Monday

Tuesday

Wednesday

 Thursday

 Friday

 Saturday

 Sunday

Monday

Tuesday

Wednesday

 Thursday

 Friday

 Saturday

 Sunday

 Monday

 Tuesday

 Wednesday

Week Forty-Six

 Thursday

 Friday

 Saturday

 Sunday

 Monday

 Tuesday

 Wednesday

 Thursday

 Friday

 Saturday

 Sunday

Monday

Tuesday

Wednesday

 Thursday

 Friday

 Saturday

 Sunday

Monday

Tuesday

Wednesday

Week Forty-Nine

 Thursday

 Friday

 Saturday

 Sunday

Monday

Tuesday

Wednesday

Week Fifty

 Thursday

 Friday

 Saturday

 Sunday

 Monday

 Tuesday

 Wednesday

 Thursday

 Friday

 Saturday

 Sunday

 Monday

 Tuesday

 Wednesday

Thursday

Friday

Saturday

Sunday

YOU HAVE THE TIME!

We all have 24 hours a day.

Can you wake an hour earlier to write a chapter in your book? To work out?

Where are your breaks, naps and meals?

If you stay on schedule, how many hours do you have left to do whatever you want?

Don't forget to factor in "free time" for yourself.

Start your schedule from when you wake up. If you want to get something accomplished, you change your schedule to fit it in.

SAMPLE SCHEDULE:
4:30AM – Wake Up, Shower & Breakfast
5:30AM - Workout
6:00AM - Get ready for work
6:30AM - Commute, Work, Commute Home
6:30PM - Dinner, Quality Time with Family
8:00 Kids Bed, Write a Chapter in my Book
10:00 Bedtime for Me

Making the time, add focus and consistency; just imagine what you can do if you give yourself a chance!
NOW IT'S YOUR TURN!

Important Notes

Important Notes

Important Notes

Important Notes

Important Notes

Important Notes

Important Notes

Important Notes

Now that we're friends, let's help each other with our goals!

Text "FriendInMyHead" to 31996
for encouraging texts from Birdie!

&

Join Our Secret Facebook Group:

https://www.facebook.com/groups/FriendInMyHead/

Thank you for taking this journey with Birdie!

Within her writing and publishing company, Miss Birdie's Books, Inc.; Birdie Chesson offers writing, lifestyle & book coaching services, helping many people worldwide.

If you're interested in coaching, hosting or attending one of Birdie's workshops,

Reach us at BookCoachBirdie@gmail.com

To find out more about Birdie, her events and updates
Visit: *www.BirdieChesson.com*

www.ingramcontent.com/pod-product-compliance
Lightning Source LLC
Chambersburg PA
CBHW060740050426

42449CB00008B/1274